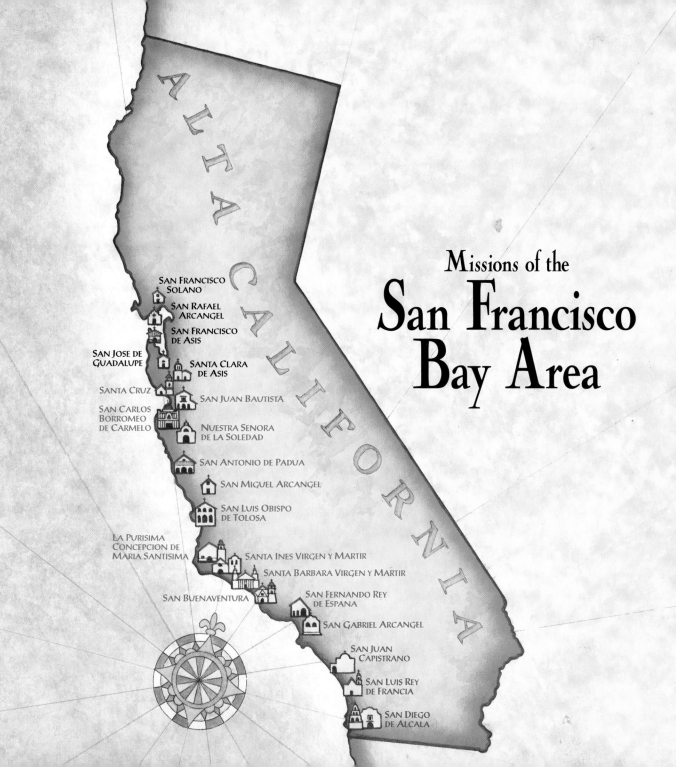

ALTA CALIFORNIA

Missions of the
San Francisco Bay Area

San Francisco
Solano

San Rafael
Arcangel

San Francisco
de Asis

San Jose de
Guadalupe

Santa Clara
de Asis

Santa Cruz

San Juan Bautista

San Carlos
Borromeo
de Carmelo

Nuestra Senora
de la Soledad

San Antonio de Padua

San Miguel Arcangel

San Luis Obispo
de Tolosa

La Purisima
Concepcion de
Maria Santisima

Santa Ines Virgen y Martir

Santa Barbara Virgen y Martir

San Buenaventura

San Fernando Rey
de Espana

San Gabriel Arcangel

San Juan
Capistrano

San Luis Rey
de Francia

San Diego
de Alcala

California
MISSIONS

Missions of the
San Francisco
Bay Area

Tekla N. White

LERNER PUBLICATIONS COMPANY

Series editors: Karen Chernyaev, Elizabeth Verdick, Mary M. Rodgers
Series photo researcher: Amy Cox
Series designer: Zachary Marell

The author dedicates this book to her daughters, Lara and Alyssa.

Every effort has been made to secure permission for the quoted material and for the photographs in this book.

LIBRARY OF CONGRESS CATALOGING-IN-PUBLICATION DATA

White, Tekla N.
    Missions of the San Francisco Bay Area / by Tekla N. White
        p. cm. — (California missions)
    Includes index.
    Summary: Charts the histories of the misisons of San Francisco de Asís, Santa Clara, San José, San Rafael Arcángel, and San Francisco Solano, and briefly describes life among the Ohlone and Coast Miwok Indians before the arrival of the Spaniards.
    ISBN 0–8225–1926–7 (lib. bdg.)
    1. Spanish mission buildings—California—San Francisco Bay Area—Juvenile literature.
2. San Francisco Bay Area (Calif.)—History, Local—Juvenile literature. [1. Missions—California. 2. California—History. 3. Costanoan Indians—Missions—California. 4. Miwok Indians—Missions—California. 5. Indians of North America—Missions—California.] I. Title. II. Series.
F868.S156W43 1996
979.4'6—dc20
                                                                            95–8714
                                                                            CIP
                                                                            AC
Manufactured in the United States of America   Rev.
1 2 3 4 5 6 – JR – 01 00 99 98 97 96

Cover: **Palm trees and wisteria (a flowering vine) frame the bell tower of Mission Santa Clara de Asís.** *Title page:* **A mosaic (tiled artwork) in San Francisco de Asís shows the arrival of the San Carlos, a supply ship, at the mission.**

CONTENTS

GLOSSARY

adobe: A type of clay soil found in Mexico and in dry parts of the United States. In Alta California, workers formed wet adobe into bricks that hardened in the sun.

Alta California (Upper California): An old Spanish name for the present-day state of California.

Baja California (Lower California): A strip of land off the northwestern coast of Mexico that lies between the Pacific Ocean and the Gulf of California. Part of Mexico, Baja California borders the U.S. state of California.

Franciscan: A member of the Order of Friars Minor, a Roman Catholic community founded in Italy by Saint Francis of Assisi in 1209. The Franciscans are dedicated to performing missionary work and acts of charity.

mission: A center where missionaries (religious teachers) work to spread their beliefs to other people and to teach a new way of life.

missionary: A person sent out by a religious group to spread its beliefs to other people.

neophyte: A Greek word meaning "newly converted" that refers to an Indian baptized into the Roman Catholic community.

New Spain: A large area once belonging to Spain that included what are now the southwestern United States and Mexico. After 1821, when New Spain had gained its independence from the Spanish Empire, the region became known as the Republic of Mexico.

presidio: A Spanish fort for housing soldiers. In Alta California, Spaniards built presidios to protect the missions and priests from possible attacks and to enforce order in the region. California's four main presidios were located at San Diego, Santa Barbara, Monterey, and San Francisco.

quadrangle: A four-sided enclosure surrounded by buildings.

reservation: Tracts of land set aside by the U.S. government to be used by Native Americans.

secularization: A series of laws enacted by the Mexican government in the 1830s. The rulings aimed to take mission land and buildings from Franciscan control and to place the churches in the hands of parish priests, who didn't perform missionary work. Much of the land was distributed to families and individuals.

PRONUNCIATION GUIDE*

Anza, Juan Bautista de	AHN-sah, WAHN baw-TEES-tah day
Argüello, Luís Antonio	ar-GWAY-oh, loo-EES ahn-TOH-nyo
El Camino Reál	el kah-MEE-no ray-AHL
Estanislao	ays-tah-nees-LAOW
Lasuén, Fermín de	lah-soo-AYN, fair-MEEN day
Miwok	MEE-wahk
Ohlone	oh-LOH-nee
Pico, Pío	PEE-koh, PEE-oh
Quijas, José Lorenzo	KEE-hahs, hoh-SAY loh-REHN-soh
San Francisco de Asís	SAHN frahn SEES-koh day ah-SEES
San Francisco Solano	SAHN frahn SEES-koh soh-LAHN-oh
San José de Guadalupe	SAHN hoh-SAY day (g)wah-dah-LOO-pay
San Rafael Arcángel	SAHN rah-fah-AYL ahr-KAHN-hel
Santa Clara de Asís	SAHN-tah KLAH-rah day ah-SEES
Serra, Junípero	SEH-rrah, hoo-NEE-pay-roh
Vallejo, Mariano Guadalupe	vah-YAY-hoh, mah-ree-AH-noh (g)wah-dah-LOO-pay

* Local pronunciations may differ.

PREFACE

The religious beliefs and traditions of the Indians of California teach that the blessings of a rich land and a mild climate are gifts from the Creator. The Indians show their love and respect for the Creator—and for all of creation—by carefully managing the land for future generations and by living in harmony with the natural environment.

Over the course of many centuries, the Indians of California organized small, independent societies. Only in the hot, dry deserts of southeastern California did they farm the land to feed themselves. Elsewhere, the abundance of fish, deer, antelope, waterfowl, and wild seeds supplied all that the Indians needed for survival. The economies of these societies did not create huge surpluses of food. Instead the people produced only what they expected would meet their needs. Yet there is no record of famine during the long period when Indians in California managed the land.

These age-old beliefs and practices stood in sharp contrast to the policies of the Spaniards who began to settle areas of California in the late 1700s. Spain established religious missions along the coast to anchor its empire in California. At these missions, Spanish priests baptized thousands of Indians into the Roman Catholic religion. Instead of continuing to hunt and gather their food, the Indians were made to work on mission estates where farming supported the settlements. Pastures for mission livestock soon took over Indian land, and European farming activities depleted native plants. Illnesses that the Spaniards had unintentionally carried from Europe brought additional suffering to many Indian groups.

The Indians living in California numbered 340,000 in the late 1700s, but only 100,000 remained after roughly 70 years of Spanish missionization. Many of the Indians died from disease. Spanish soldiers killed other Indians during native revolts at the missions. Some entire Indian societies were wiped out.

Thousands of mission Indian descendants proudly continue to practice their native culture and to speak their native language. But what is most important to these survivors is that their people's history be understood by those who now call California home, as well as by others across the nation. Through this series of books, young readers will learn for the first time how the missions affected the Indians and their traditional societies.

Perhaps one of the key lessons to be learned from an honest and evenhanded account of California's missions is that the Indians had something important to teach the Spaniards and the people who came to the region later. Our ancestors and today's elders instill in us that we must respect and live in harmony with animals, plants, and one another. While this is an ancient wisdom, it seems especially relevant to our future survival.

Professor Edward D. Castillo
Cahuilla-Luiseño Mission Indian Descendant

INTRODUCTION

FOUNDED BY SPAIN, THE CALIFORNIA **MISSIONS** ARE located on a narrow strip of California's Pacific coast. Some of the historic buildings sit near present-day Highway 101, which roughly follows what was once a roadway called El Camino Reál (the Royal Road), so named to honor the king of Spain. The trail linked a chain of 21 missions set up between 1769 and 1823.

Spain, along with leaders of the Roman Catholic Church, established missions and *presidios* (forts) throughout the Spanish Empire to strengthen its claim to the land. In the 1600s, Spain built mission settlements on the peninsula known as **Baja California,** as well as in other areas of **New Spain** (present-day Mexico).

The goal of the Spanish mission system in North America was to make Indians accept Spanish ways and become loyal subjects of the Spanish king. Priests functioning as **missionaries** (religious teachers) tried to convert the local Indian populations to Catholicism and to

In the mid-1700s, Native Americans living in what is now California came into contact with Roman Catholic missionaries from Spain.

11

When a new mission was established, a priest said mass for the soldiers and Indian onlookers.

teach them to dress and behave like Spaniards. Soldiers came to protect the missionaries and to make sure the Indians obeyed the priests.

During the late 1700s, Spain wanted to spread its authority northward from Baja California into the region known as **Alta California,** where Spain's settlement pattern would be repeated. The first group of Spanish soldiers and missionaries traveled to Alta California in 1769. The missionaries, priests of the **Franciscan** order, were led by Junípero Serra, the father-president of the mission system.

The soldiers and missionaries came into contact with communities of Native Americans, or Indians, that dotted the coastal and inland areas of Alta California. For thousands of years, the region had been home to many Native American groups that spoke a wide variety of languages. Using these Indians as unpaid laborers was vital to the success of the mission system. The mission economy was based on agriculture—a way of life unfamiliar to local Indians, who mostly hunted game and gathered wild plants for food.

Although some Indians willingly joined the missions, the Franciscans relied on various methods to convince or force other Native Americans to become part of the mission system. The priests sometimes lured Indians with gifts of glass beads and colored cloth or other items new to the Native Americans. Some Indians who lost their hunting and food-gathering grounds to mission farms and ranches joined the Spanish settlements to survive. In other cases, Spanish soldiers forcibly took villagers from their homes.

Neophytes, or Indians recruited into the missions, were expected to learn the Catholic faith and the skills for farming and building. Afterward—Spain reasoned—the Native Americans would be able to manage the property themselves, a process that officials figured would take 10 years. But a much different turn of events took place.

Highlights of Present-Day California

- • City
- ⛪ Mission (see list below left)
- County
- El Camino Reál
- U.S. highway

Miles
0 20 40 60 80 100

0 40 80 120
Kilometers

NEVADA

Sacramento
Sacramento River

A Sonoma
San Pablo Bay
Bodega Bay
B
San Rafael
SAN FRANCISCO PRESIDIO
San Francisco
Alcatraz I.
C
Fremont
D
San Francisco Bay
E
San Jose
Santa Clara
Guadalupe R.
F
San Lorenzo R.
Pajaro R.
G
Santa Cruz
Monterey Bay
San Juan Bautista
MONTEREY PRESIDIO
Monterey
Carmel
H
Carmel R.
Salinas R.
I
Soledad
King City
San Antonio R.
Nacimiento R.
J
San Antonio R.
K
San Miguel
101
SIERRA NEVADA
Stanislaus R.
San Joaquin River
San Joaquin Valley
CALIFORNIA
COAST RANGE

PACIFIC OCEAN

L
San Luis Obispo
La Purisima
Lompoc
M
N
Solvang
Santa Ynez
Santa Ynez R.
Point Conception
O
Santa Barbara
SANTA BARBARA PRESIDIO
SANTA BARBARA CHANNEL
Ventura R.
P
Ventura
VENTURA COUNTY
Santa Clara R.
Q
San Fernando
R
San Gabriel R.
San Gabriel
San Ana R.
Los Angeles R.
Santa Monica Bay
5
Los Angeles
ORANGE COUNTY
S
San Juan Capistrano
T
Oceanside
U
San Diego
SAN DIEGO PRESIDIO
San Diego R.
San Diego Bay

MOJAVE DESERT

N

San Miguel I.
Santa Rosa I.
Santa Cruz I.
Anacapa Is.
SANTA BARBARA ISLANDS
Santa Barbara I.
San Nicolas I.
Santa Catalina I.
San Clemente I.

UNITED STATES
MEXICO
BAJA CALIFORNIA
M E X I C O

PACIFIC OCEAN

⛪ **CALIFORNIA MISSIONS**

A   San Francisco Solano
B   San Rafael Arcángel
C   San Francisco de Asís
D   San José de Guadalupe
E   Santa Clara de Asís
F   Santa Cruz
G   San Juan Bautista
H   San Carlos Borromeo
I   Soledad
J   San Antonio de Padua
K   San Miguel Arcángel
L   San Luis Obispo
M   La Purísima
N   Santa Inés
O   Santa Bárbara
P   San Buenaventura
Q   San Fernando Rey
R   San Gabriel Arcángel
S   San Juan Capistrano
T   San Luis Rey de Francia
U   San Diego de Alcalá

California Mission	Founding Date
San Diego de Alcalá	*July 16, 1769*
San Carlos Borromeo de Carmelo	*June 3, 1770*
San Antonio de Padua	*July 14, 1771*
San Gabriel Arcángel	*September 8, 1771*
San Luis Obispo de Tolosa	*September 1, 1772*
San Francisco de Asís	*June 29, 1776*
San Juan Capistrano	*November 1, 1776*
Santa Clara de Asís	*January 12, 1777*
San Buenaventura	*March 31, 1782*
Santa Bárbara Virgen y Mártir	*December 4, 1786*
La Purísima Concepción de Maria Santísima	*December 8, 1787*
Santa Cruz	*August 28, 1791*
Nuestra Señora de la Soledad	*October 9, 1791*
San José de Guadalupe	*June 11, 1797*
San Juan Bautista	*June 24, 1797*
San Miguel Arcángel	*July 25, 1797*
San Fernando Rey de España	*September 8, 1797*
San Luis Rey de Francia	*June 13, 1798*
Santa Inés Virgen y Mártir	*September 17, 1804*
San Rafael Arcángel	*December 14, 1817*
San Francisco Solano	*July 4, 1823*

Forced to abandon their villages and to give up their age-old traditions, many Native Americans didn't adjust to mission life. In fact, most Indians died soon after entering the missions—mainly from European diseases that eventually killed thousands of Indians throughout California.

Because hundreds of Indian laborers worked at each mission, most of the settlements thrived. The missions produced grapes, olives, wheat, cattle hides, cloth, soap, candles, and other goods. In fact, the missions successfully introduced to Alta California a variety of crops and livestock that still benefit present-day Californians.

The missions became so productive that the Franciscans established a valuable trade net-

A bell (facing page) placed along El Camino Reál sits outside Mission San Rafael Arcángel.

work. Mission priests exchanged goods and provided nearby soldiers and settlers with provisions. The agricultural wealth of the missions angered many settlers and soldiers, who resented the priests for holding Alta California's most fertile land and the majority of the livestock and for controlling the Indian labor force.

This resentment grew stronger after 1821, when New Spain became the independent country of Mexico. Mexico claimed Alta California and began the **secularization** of the missions. The mission churches still offered religious services, but the Spanish Franciscans were to be replaced by secular priests. These priests weren't missionaries seeking to convert people.

By 1836 the neophytes were free to leave the missions, and the settlements quickly declined from the loss of workers. Few of the former neophytes found success away from the missions, however. Many continued as forced laborers on *ranchos* (ranches) or in nearby *pueblos* (towns), earning little or no pay.

In 1848 Mexico lost a war against the United States and ceded Alta California to the U.S. government. By that time, about half of Alta California's Indian population had died. Neophytes who had remained at the missions often had no village to which to return. They moved to pueblos or to inland areas. Meanwhile, the missions went into a state of decay, only to be rebuilt years later.

This book covers the 5 missions located in the San Francisco Bay area, the northernmost region settled by the Franciscans. Of the 21 missions, San Francisco de Asís was built sixth, Santa Clara de Asís eighth, and San José de Guadalupe fourteenth. Missions San Rafael Arcángel and San Francisco Solano were the last to be established. These missions were set up in areas well populated by Indians, especially the Ohlone and the Coast Miwok.

15

PART ONE

Early Life along the Coast

THE TULE GRASS SWAYED, WHISPERING TO THE afternoon winds that blew ripples across the marsh waters. The songs and laughter of women pounding acorns mingled with the cries of the long-necked geese that crossed the sky. In villages along the shores of the great bay and its lagoons, young and old gathered around storytellers who recited ancient tales.

For thousands of years, the area around San Francisco Bay in northern California was the land of the Ohlone and the Coast Miwok Indians. It was here, the Native American storytellers explained, that their people were created. This place near the ocean had always been their home.

Called the Golden Gate, the Pacific entrance to San Francisco Bay is often shrouded in fog. Before eighteenth-century explorers charted the bay on a map, ships cruising the area unknowingly sailed past the natural harbor.

Ohlone Indians lived south of the bay along the Pacific Ocean. North of the bay lay the territory of the Coast Miwok people. The bay and lands inhabited by other tribes separated the Coast Miwok from the Ohlone. The two groups sometimes met to trade goods but otherwise had little contact.

The Ohlone

The land of the Ohlone was like a sponge, soaking up the rains that fell during the wet season, from October through April.

The rainwater fed the nearby streams, ponds, marshes, and underground springs. It also nourished a wide variety of plants and animals. For this reason, the Ohlone almost always had enough food.

Early in the fall, before the wet season set in, oak trees in the hills provided acorns—a staple food source. Men and boys climbed the trees and shook acorns from the branches for the women and girls to collect. The Native Americans ground these nuts to make flour for bread and porridge.

From the ocean, the Ohlone gathered a seaweed called kelp. They scooped mussels, abalone, and clams from the sandy coast. Streams supplied the Ohlone with freshwater fish. In the

The Ohlone removed acorn skins by winnowing, or tossing the shelled acorns into the air and catching them in a basket (above). With each toss, bits of nut skin blew away. The Indians stored much of the harvest in huge baskets, or granaries (left).

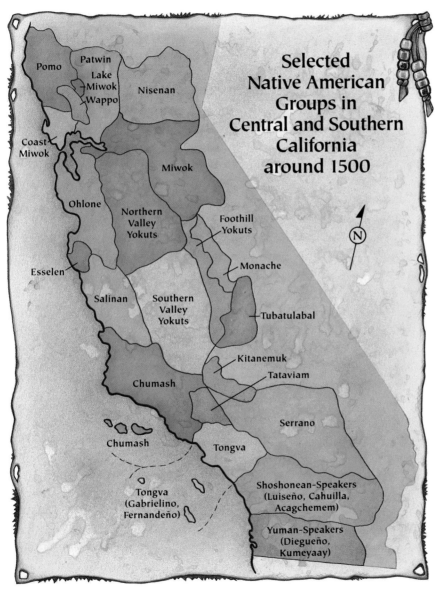

Selected Native American Groups in Central and Southern California around 1500

Pomo
Patwin
Lake Miwok
Wappo
Nisenan
Coast Miwok
Miwok
Ohlone
Northern Valley Yokuts
Foothill Yokuts
Monache
Esselen
Salinan
Southern Valley Yokuts
Tubatulabal
Kitanemuk
Tataviam
Chumash
Serrano
Chumash
Tongva
Tongva (Gabrielino, Fernandeño)
Shoshonean-Speakers (Luiseño, Cahuilla, Acagchemem)
Yuman-Speakers (Diegueño, Kumeyaay)

N

marshes, hunters used straw decoys to lure ducks and geese into nets.

The Ohlone feasted on wild berries, gooseberries, pine nuts, and roasted grasshoppers. In the winter, villagers looked for edible mushrooms and in the spring picked clover, mustard, and other herbs.

Because the climate around the bay was usually mild, though often damp, the Ohlone had little need for clothing. Women wore skirts made from dried grass or from tules (marsh reeds) and deerskin. When the weather grew cold, both men and women dressed in rabbit-fur cloaks. Except for the cloaks, men usually didn't wear clothing.

In Ohlone society, a chief ruled over a small tribal grouping, which included a number of villages. The tribal chief followed the rules and traditions of the group, giving speeches and advice to help people solve their problems.

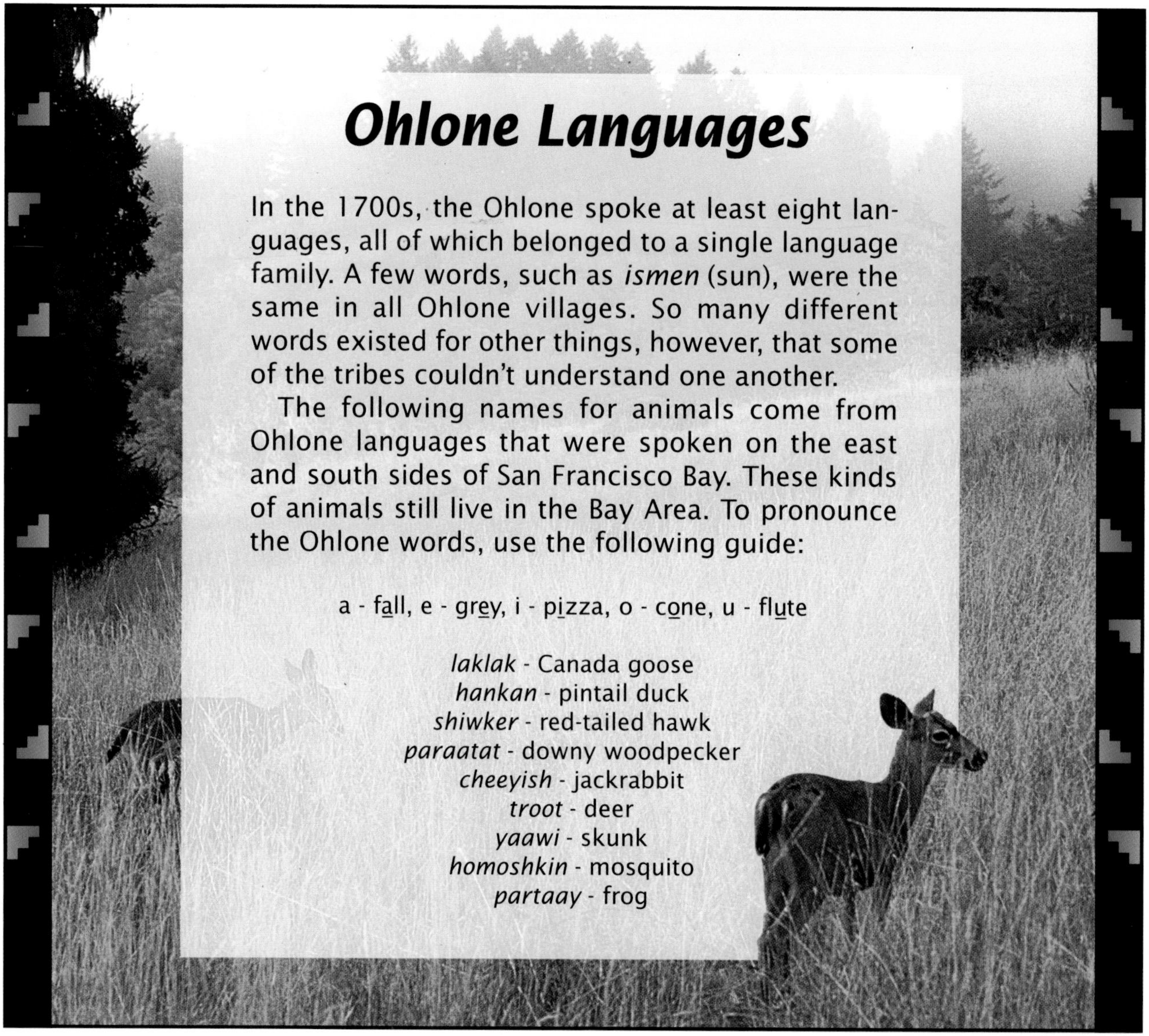

Ohlone Languages

In the 1700s, the Ohlone spoke at least eight languages, all of which belonged to a single language family. A few words, such as *ismen* (sun), were the same in all Ohlone villages. So many different words existed for other things, however, that some of the tribes couldn't understand one another.

The following names for animals come from Ohlone languages that were spoken on the east and south sides of San Francisco Bay. These kinds of animals still live in the Bay Area. To pronounce the Ohlone words, use the following guide:

a - f<u>a</u>ll, e - gr<u>e</u>y, i - p<u>i</u>zza, o - c<u>o</u>ne, u - fl<u>u</u>te

laklak - Canada goose
hankan - pintail duck
shiwker - red-tailed hawk
paraatat - downy woodpecker
cheeyish - jackrabbit
troot - deer
yaawi - skunk
homoshkin - mosquito
partaay - frog

The chief—as well as all other adults in the group—was responsible for the education and behavior of Ohlone children. Adults in the village showed young girls and boys how to behave by example. Storytellers taught children age-old tribal beliefs through myths and legends.

The Coast Miwok

The Coast Miwok lived near the ocean, where waves pounded at high cliffs alive with screeching gulls. Villages stretched across warm valleys. Smoke from small cooking fires drifted from cone-shaped homes toward the hills and mountains farther inland.

The Coast Miwok also could find abundant food resources. Like the Ohlone, the Coast Miwok collected acorns to make porridge and bread. The people gathered pepperwoods, a fruit from which they produced a chocolaty drink. In the summer, the Native Americans moved to the hills, where deer, rabbits, and berries were more plentiful.

Ocean waves swept ashore kelp, mussels, clams, and crabs, which the Coast Miwok collected. From tule canoes, the

Expert fishermen, Coast Miwok were able to spear salmon and other fish with ease.

Native Americans netted salmon and eels. Armed with spears and basket traps, the men caught fish in shallow ponds.

The Coast Miwok had what they needed for survival. But to acquire additional items unavailable in their area, the Coast Miwok traded with other tribes. Traders from distant and nearby territories brought valuable minerals, stones, and plants—materials the Coast Miwok used for tools, weapons, and medicine.

The Coast Miwok also bargained for yellow paint and for obsidian. This shiny, black volcanic rock came from the Sierra Nevada, a mountain range to the east. The Native Americans fashioned obsidian into cutting tools and arrowheads. The Coast Miwok exchanged clamshell beads, fish, and other local products for the goods they needed.

Sometimes the Coast Miwok traveled northward into the lands of other tribes to collect turtles, tobacco, and medicinal plants.

Tule Canoes

The Coast Miwok made canoes from bundled, dry tule reeds. Both ends of the boats pointed upward. The Native Americans steered the canoes with double-bladed, wooden paddles. The crafts glided across the bay, even in choppy water. Instead of rocking the boat, waves passed through the bundles of tules, giving paddlers a smooth but damp ride.

Tule canoes still cruise San Francisco Bay. Volunteers at Coyote Hills—a park in Fremont, California—have made five of the boats. The builders cut, dried, and bundled the tules, then tied them together with about 1,500 feet of rope made from vines. *Kon Tule V,* one of these tule boats, weighs 300 pounds. Six people can ride in this 27-foot-long bundle of reeds.

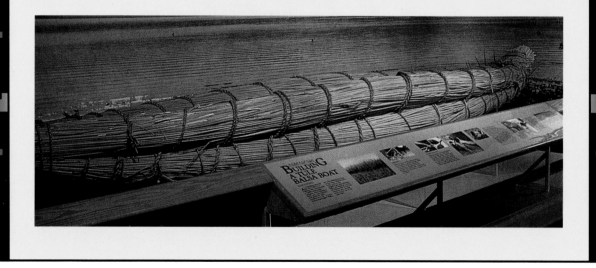

The temescal was a pit dug four or five feet into the ground and covered with a rounded roof made of brush, grass, and soil.

For the right to gather these items, the Coast Miwok allowed northern groups to fish and to dig for clams near the bay.

The Coast Miwok took time from their trading, food gathering, and other work to cleanse the spirit and the body. Miwok men, for example, used the temescal (sweat lodge) as a place to purify and strengthen themselves for a deer hunt.

A small fire in the center of the lodge produced intense heat, which caused the men to sweat heavily. Afterward, the men bathed in a river.

Coast Miwok villagers also found time for games. Athletes competed in a form of hockey, using a wooden ball. Children played with dolls made of mud and sticks or challenged one another in a game similar to jacks.

The Coast Miwok celebrated most occasions with dances and songs. The Indians staged dances to cure ill people. There were dances for hunting bear and deer, for netting salmon, and for the acorn harvest. Dancers moved to the sounds of clappers, rattles, and whistles. During special events, some villagers performed as clowns, magicians, and fire-eaters.

The Coast Miwok and the Ohlone shared a respect for the land that provided them with the resources they needed to survive. Homelands were sacred to the Native Americans. Their well-being rested in part on knowing that the earth would always support them.

European Contact

In the late 1500s, Spanish and English explorers landed in Alta California. Few, however, ventured far up the coast. In 1579 Sir Francis Drake sailed to northern Alta California. He traded gifts with Native Americans, possibly the Coast Miwok, and claimed the region for England.

Meanwhile, Spanish explorers had staked a similar claim for the king of Spain, adding Alta California to the territory of New Spain. The various visitors to Alta California didn't stay. They simply made their claims and returned home.

During the 1700s, Spain began to suspect Russia and Britain of wanting to send settlers to Alta California. To strengthen its claim to the land, Spain decided to establish its own settlements

English pirate and explorer Sir Francis Drake probably met Coast Miwok Indians when he anchored his ship, the Golden Hind, *off the Pacific coast in 1579.*

A Catholic priest blesses two Franciscans headed for the missions in Alta California. Few Franciscan priests were willing to leave the comforts of Spain for an isolated life in the remote outpost.

Junípero Serra (1713–1784) founded nine of the twenty-one Franciscan missions in Alta California. Other priests of the Franciscan order praised Serra highly for his strong faith and for his devotion to missionary work.

on the coast. But these settlements needed people.

Instead of convincing Spaniards to move to Alta California, Spanish officials intended to make the Indians in the region loyal Spanish subjects. Spain planned to accomplish this goal with the help of missionaries from the Catholic Church. These priests would be directed by Father Junípero Serra, a leading member of the Franciscan religious order.

To become Spanish subjects, the Indians would have to practice Catholicism, the religion of Spain. Father Serra's role involved setting up a series of missions along the coast of Alta California. The missions would be centers for converting the Native Americans to Catholicism and for teaching them a new way of life.

Franciscan priests posted at each of the mission sites would try to get nearby Native Americans to undergo baptism. This ritual, performed with water, welcomed a person into a religious community. After being baptized, the Indians were called neophytes.

Under the plan, the neophytes would live and work at the missions as unpaid laborers. Soldiers stationed at the missions would protect the priests from possible Indian resistance.

The first mission was established at San Diego, far south of the Bay Area. Meanwhile, Captain Gaspar de Portolá headed an expedition to find Monterey Bay for the next mission site. He used as a guide an old description of the bay that proved to be faulty.

The soldiers crossed hills and canyons, clearing their way through forests with pickaxes, crowbars, and spades. Portolá bypassed Monterey only to stumble upon the great bay, named San Francisco (Saint Francis) by the Spaniards. Ohlone Indians near the great bay gave the explorers acorn flour and black seeds to eat before the expedition returned to San Diego.

In the following years, other Spanish explorers led several expeditions to the San Francisco Bay area. They learned that the bay made an excellent natural harbor. The travelers met with

> *THE EXPEDITION MADE ITS WAY NORTHWARD THROUGH SAND DUNES, THORNY BRAMBLES, AND CACTI, SURVIVING DUST STORMS, BITTER COLD, AND LACK OF WATER.*

the Ohlone to see if the Indians were friendly. The Spaniards recommended that the Bay Area be the site of the third mission.

The Anza Expedition

By September 1775, Captain Juan Bautista de Anza had or-

ganized an expedition. Anza prepared to take 34 families overland from New Spain to San Francisco Bay. The families were to establish a pueblo called Yerba Buena (present-day San Francisco) near the new mission, San Francisco de Asís.

The Spanish government provided the group with necessities such as horses, mules, livestock, food, and clothing. The expedition included children, soldiers, muleteers to care for the pack animals, *vaqueros* (cowboys) to tend the cattle, Native American interpreters, and servants for the priests.

On October 23, after much preparation, the travelers left New Spain on horseback. The expedition made its way northward through sand dunes, thorny brambles, and cacti, surviving dust storms, bitter cold, and lack of water. In March 1776, in spite of mud and heavy rains along the Pacific coast, the travelers reached the mission at Monterey. Here they waited while a site was selected for their pueblo.

Anza soon left Monterey to explore the area that is now the city of San Francisco. He selected sites for the new mission, for a presidio, and for a pueblo. Lieutenant José Moraga made plans to transport the settlers and supplies from Monterey to San Francisco.

On June 3, a vessel named the *San Carlos* docked in Monterey with carpenters and supplies for the new settlement at San Francisco. Two weeks later, Moraga and the settlers began their overland journey to San Francisco Bay. The *San Carlos* sailed up the coast.

Moraga's group reached its destination in late June and built a bower of branches to serve as a temporary chapel. Father Francisco Palóu, the priest in charge of the mission, said the first mass.

Meanwhile, the sailors on the *San Carlos* were battling fierce

Captain Juan Bautista de Anza and the group of settlers who came with him faced many hardships on their way to San Francisco Bay.

winds and disease. The ship eventually reached San Francisco Bay—nearly two months after Moraga did.

After the building supplies and carpenters arrived, Father Palóu ordered the construction of more permanent structures. Soldiers, sailors, and Christian Indians from other missions did most of the work. By mid-September, the workers had raised a village of **adobe** (mud-brick) houses. Crews made the church out of wood and roofed it with mud and tules.

On October 9, 1776, Father Palóu dedicated Mission San Francisco de Asís, the sixth Franciscan mission in Alta California. After Father Palóu said mass, the ship's crew fired guns and cannons. The loud explosions frightened some of the Ohlone, who had come from a nearby village to watch the scene. They left and didn't return for several months.

PART TWO

Missions of the San Francisco Bay Area

ALTHOUGH THE FRANCISCAN MISSIONS OF THE SAN Francisco Bay area were built to serve the same purpose, each has its own history. The first mission built in the Bay Area—San Francisco de Asís—had trouble gaining and keeping neophytes. Santa Clara, on the other hand, averaged the highest number of neophytes over a 25-year period and proved to be one of the most productive missions. (No discussion of why.)

Mission San José was the birthplace of Estanislao, a neophyte who successfully led other Indians in a rebellion against mission soldiers. San Rafael Arcángel, which at first functioned as a branch

The restored San José overlooks the mission's graveyard.

Grassland near the San Francisco Bay provided the Franciscans with grazing ground for their cattle.

of San Francisco de Asís, was originally a hospital. San Francisco Solano was the only mission established after Spain no longer ruled Alta California, at a time when the Franciscans were losing their authority.

Mission San Francisco de Asís

After the dedication of Mission San Francisco in 1776, work continued on the mission and on the pueblo. Workers constructed more buildings and plowed the land. The Californios, the name given to Spanish-speaking settlers in Alta California, dug a ditch to carry water from a stream to the fields where crops had been planted.

To be able to identify its cattle, each mission created a branding symbol. Using a hierro, or branding iron, cowboys burned the mark onto the livestock. The symbol for San Francisco de Asís was the letter F.

From the mission, the priests could see the Ohlone hunting ducks and paddling tule boats in the bay. Some Ohlone went to the mission to trade ducks for beads and food. But many Indians wanted the newcomers to leave Ohlone territory. The Native Americans felt uneasy about the soldiers, who carried guns.

On one visit to the mission, several Ohlone threatened a Spaniard. To prevent further resistance, soldiers whipped the Indians. The Ohlone stayed away from the mission for several months after the beatings.

Working and Living Conditions

Almost a year had passed before the Franciscans baptized any Ohlone. The priests convinced some Native Americans to join the mission by giving them glass beads and other gifts.

After the Indians were baptized, the priests did not allow the neophytes to return permanently to their old homes. Soldiers forcibly brought back Native Americans who visited their villages for too long. The missionaries feared that if the neophytes lived in their villages,

The Ohlone often wore feathered headdresses for special Indian ceremonies.

they would abandon their mission work and European ways.

The success of San Francisco de Asís depended in part on using neophytes as an unpaid workforce. The neophytes tended crops and livestock, produced goods, and constructed buildings. When neophytes were not laboring, they were usually learning the Catholic faith.

By the late 1700s, so many Indians were living at the mission that the priests needed a larger church and a greater food supply. Neophytes began work on a new church. They also tore down the mission buildings, which covered fertile soil, to make room for more farmland.

For the new church, the neophytes made thick adobe walls. The Indians cut timber from nearby redwood trees to form the roof. Wooden pegs carved from manzanita bushes took the place of nails. Workers then covered the roof with rounded tiles made from dried clay.

Inside the church, the Franciscans wrapped the ceiling beams with tightly stretched pieces of canvas. The neophytes used vegetable dyes and clay to paint red, gray, white, and yellow chevrons (V-shaped stripes) on the beams. Wooden statues of Catholic saints and a hand-carved altar edged with gold leaf decorated the interior. The face of the church eventually featured a wooden balcony, three bells, and six short columns.

The new church, which was ready for use in 1791, sat at one end of the mission's **quadrangle.** The quadrangle was made up of buildings that enclosed a patio area on four sides. The structures housed workshops, storage rooms, and the priests' living quarters.

In the surrounding fields, neophytes learned to plow and cultivate wheat, corn, and barley. The Indians also cared for horses, mules, and herds of cattle and sheep. Some men became blacksmiths, carpenters, and tailors. Others made adobe bricks and roof tiles for mission buildings. Neophyte women learned to spin wool, to weave, and to make soap and candles.

Although work went forward at Mission San Francisco de Asís, the mission's labor force was suffering. Most neophytes longed to return to their old lifestyles. They wanted to hunt, to fish, and to gather food. They missed their traditional religious ceremonies and the ability to travel freely.

In addition, many neophytes died from measles and smallpox,

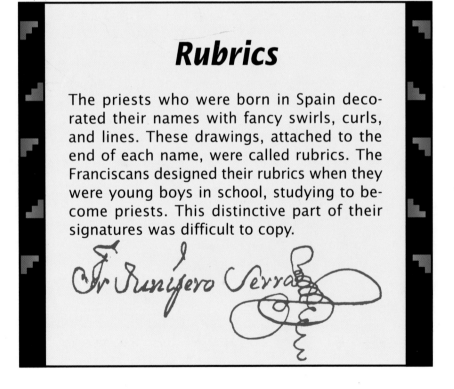

Rubrics

The priests who were born in Spain decorated their names with fancy swirls, curls, and lines. These drawings, attached to the end of each name, were called rubrics. The Franciscans designed their rubrics when they were young boys in school, studying to become priests. This distinctive part of their signatures was difficult to copy.

diseases the Spaniards had carried to the region. Poor sanitation added to the health problems of these Indians, who shared cramped quarters where germs spread easily.

Away from their traditional villages, the neophytes no longer had access to temescals and to their own healers, or shamans. The Franciscans learned as much as they could about curing disease from medical books, but hundreds of neophytes continued to die from European diseases every year.

Ohlone who joined the mission sometimes suffered from malnutrition. Meals at Mission San Francisco de Asís weren't as nourishing or as varied as the traditional Native American diet. The priests used mainly wheat, one of the mission's more successful crops, to make a filling cereal. Because the mission often had an abundance of wheat, the neophytes usually received a breakfast of cereal, a lunch of meat and cereal, and cereal again for supper.

San Francisco de Asís is also referred to as Mission Dolores, after the name of a stream that once flowed nearby. The mission's adobe church, completed in 1791, still stands.

33

Disease and poor diet weren't the only problems the neophytes faced. The priests ordered the Indians to follow strict schedules. The ringing of the mission bells signaled when the neophytes worked, prayed, and ate.

Spanish soldiers beat neophytes who missed church services or who didn't work hard enough. Some priests encouraged the beatings. They saw the neophytes as children who needed regular supervision. The Franciscans also believed that the neophytes would become better Christians through suffering.

As a result of these conditions, many neophytes ran away. At one point, there weren't enough neophytes to maintain Mission San Francisco de Asís. Soldiers brought Native Americans from villages to the east and north to strengthen the mission's workforce.

Mission Santa Clara de Asís

On January 6, 1777, Lieutenant José Moraga, Father Tómas de la Peña, and a company of soldiers left San Francisco de Asís with livestock and other supplies needed to set up another mission. They traveled southward through Ohlone territory to a valley near the Guadalupe River. Here they set up a cross to signal the founding of Mission Santa Clara de Asís, named after Saint Clare. It was the eighth Franciscan mission in California.

An arbor of branches served as a temporary church, where Father Peña said the mission's first mass on January 12, 1777. Several days later, Father José Murguía, another priest assigned to Santa Clara, arrived with more cattle, tools, and some religious items.

This A-shaped symbol (left) marked thousands of cattle at Mission Santa Clara. An original wooden statue of Saint Clare (facing page) still adorns the church at Santa Clara.

Many Ohlone lived near the site of Mission Santa Clara. Few had any interest in being baptized, however, until an outbreak of disease caused many Ohlone children to become ill and die. The Franciscan priests went to the village and baptized the sick children. Soldiers then brought the surviving children to the mission. Some of the parents came as well. These Indians became the first neophytes at Mission Santa Clara.

Because most of the neophytes were infants or young children, Mission Santa Clara initially lacked an adequate labor force. The priests tilled a small section of the land themselves, and harvests were good but small. The mission depended on grains and other supplies sent by ship from New Spain.

The supply ships, however, proved to be unreliable. Sometimes they arrived late, forcing the missionaries to go without provisions or to trade with other missions. Upon delivery, the corn and meat were usually infested with worms and the flour had spilled from its sacks.

Fortunately for the missionaries, Santa Clara was located in a fertile area. After the mission had recruited enough neophytes to make a substantial labor force, the fields and orchards flourished in most years. Santa

Clara generally raised food for the neophytes, for the soldiers at the presidio in San Francisco, and to help out newly opened missions along the chain.

Pueblo San José de Guadalupe

Months after Mission Santa Clara was founded, Lieutenant Moraga led a group of people from New Spain to land near the mission. These newcomers were the first settlers of a new pueblo called San José de Guadalupe (present-day San Jose). The town was being established to increase the non-native population of Alta California.

Most of the settlers who left their homes for faraway Alta California were very poor. Some of them agreed to move because the Spanish government offered them free farmland. Other settlers were criminals banished to Alta California as punishment for their crimes.

Each family that moved to Pueblo San José received a field, a share of the grazing land, and a permit to cut wood. The newcomers built homes and farms. The settlers also constructed a dam on the Guadalupe River that supplied water for crops.

The Californios were supposed to sell any extra crops to the soldiers but hardly produced enough to feed themselves. In contrast, Santa Clara was run efficiently and had plenty of unpaid laborers. The mission provided the military, as well as the Californios, with food, livestock, clothing, and equipment.

The Mission, the Town, and the Presidio

The priests of Santa Clara and the Californios of Pueblo San José often argued. The settlers, for example, accused the mission's neophytes of stealing cattle. Disagreements also arose over grazing space. Because the

Growing Grain

Farming tools and methods were very similar at all the missions. To prepare the soil for planting, neophytes guided oxen-pulled plows that were made from tree limbs, across the fields. The tips of the plows were covered with iron so that the tool could cut into hard ground. The farmers tossed seeds of grain into the furrows and then dragged a brush or a small tree limb across the field to push the soil over the seeds.

After the grain stalks had turned a golden brown, workers harvested them by hand. Neophytes stacked loads of stalks into an oxcart and then headed for the threshing floor—a level area paved with stone. After the load of stalks was dumped on the floor, horses walked over the grains, breaking them open and releasing the kernels.

After the grain was separated from the stalks, workers tossed the kernels high into the air and caught them in baskets. The skins and dirt were blown away by the motion. Called winnowing, this method had also been used in Ohlone and Coast Miwok villages.

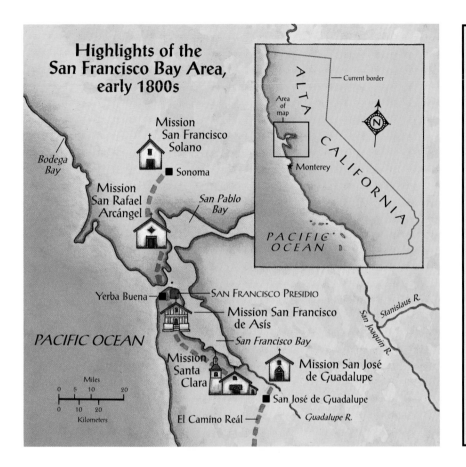

Highlights of the San Francisco Bay Area, early 1800s

Bodega Bay

Mission San Francisco Solano

Sonoma

Mission San Rafael Arcángel

San Pablo Bay

ALTA CALIFORNIA

Current border

Area of map

N

PACIFIC OCEAN

Monterey

Yerba Buena

SAN FRANCISCO PRESIDIO

Mission San Francisco de Asís

San Francisco Bay

PACIFIC OCEAN

Mission Santa Clara

Mission San José de Guadalupe

San José de Guadalupe

Stanislaus R.

San Joaquin R.

Miles
0 5 10   20

0   10   20
Kilometers

El Camino Reál

Guadalupe R.

From 1777 to 1832, 8,536 Native Americans were baptized at Mission Santa Clara—more than at any other mission. Santa Clara's records show 6,809 deaths for the same period of time. So many neophytes died that Father José Bernardo Sánchez, a priest at Santa Clara, wrote in 1830, "There is always sickness, and I'm afraid it is the end of the Indian race. What can we do?"

town was built close to the mission, the settlers' livestock often wandered onto mission land to graze. In addition, the priests and the Californios couldn't agree on how to share the water from the Guadalupe River.

Even after the mission and the pueblo settled their problems, bitter feelings continued. In the early 1800s, Santa Clara's Father Magín Catalá—as a sign of friendship—ordered 200 neophytes to clear a four-mile road from the town to the church door. The neophytes planted rows of willow trees along the path, called the

Alameda. Afterward, some of the townspeople still refused to attend the mission church.

The presidio in San Francisco had grown dependent on Mission Santa Clara for food, livestock, and skilled Indian labor. In exchange, the presidio gave cloth, iron, chocolate, silk thread, razors, nails, and axes. The soldiers, however, resented the missionaries for providing for the neophytes first. A poor mission harvest in any given year meant that the soldiers might have to do with less.

Events in New Spain began to shed a different light on the relationship between the mission, the town, and the presidio. In 1810 people in New Spain began to fight for independence from Spain. At first, this event had little impact on people living in Alta California because New Spain was far to the south.

At the same time, though, the Spanish government was losing interest in Alta California and its missions. Involved in costly wars, Spain needed to channel its money to its European-based army and navy. As a result, supply ships rarely traveled to the coast of Alta California anymore. The missions, the soldiers, and the settlers in Alta California had to increasingly rely on one another.

Mission San José de Guadalupe

In June 1797, Fermín Francisco de Lasuén, who had replaced Junípero Serra as father-president, traveled to the eastern side of San Francisco Bay in Ohlone territory. There he founded the fourteenth mission in California. He raised a cross and celebrated mass for Mission San José de Guadalupe, in honor of Saint Joseph.

The letter J marked cattle from Mission San José.

Two days after the dedication, construction of the quadrangle began. Soldiers and neophytes from nearby Mission Santa Clara built houses and a temporary wooden chapel at the new mission site. The priests of Santa Clara sent sheep and cattle. During the first year, the Franciscans baptized 33 Indians at Mission San José, an average number for a beginning mission.

Father Buenaventura Fortuni and Father Narciso Durán came to Mission San José in 1806, when the walls of the permanent church were being constructed. Under the direction of these two priests, the mission's agricultural production increased. The priests baptized hundreds of Indians, but many of the neophytes died soon afterward from European diseases.

Clashing Religions

Most missions operated successful farms and ranches. But to the Franciscans, the most important work was not agricultural but religious. They tried to convert as many Indians to Roman Catholicism as possible.

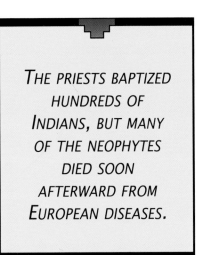

THE PRIESTS BAPTIZED HUNDREDS OF INDIANS, BUT MANY OF THE NEOPHYTES DIED SOON AFTERWARD FROM EUROPEAN DISEASES.

Several difficulties slowed the progress of the Franciscans. Language barriers, for example, made teaching the neophytes difficult. The Indians belonged to different tribes that spoke a great variety of languages and dialects—too many for the priests to learn quickly. For that reason, the priests said mass in Latin (the language used in the Catholic Church). Some prayers were taught in Spanish.

Because the Franciscans could not explain what the words meant, the neophytes didn't understand what the priests were saying. The neophytes simply repeated prayers in a language foreign to them.

By encouraging the Indians to pray like Franciscans, the priests hoped to "improve" the neophytes. Although many priests used force, they believed their methods were necessary *many did not* and proper.

Spreading the Catholic faith was important to the Franciscans, who believed strongly in the teachings of the Bible. But the Native Americans held their own religious views. Most neophytes continued to believe in the religion they had learned in their villages.

Ohlone beliefs stemmed from the Creator. People, the Ohlone said, were created by Coyote

39

An Ohlone Indian wears a traditional feathered headdress while performing a ceremonial dance. Some priests allowed neophytes to follow a few Indian traditions. But once baptized, the Indians lost much of their freedom.

after the great flood that formed the earth. But people were only part of the picture. The Ohlone believed that mountains, hills, stones, and all living creatures had spirits. As a result, all of nature was to be treated with respect. An Ohlone hunter, for example, thanked the spirit of the deer or rabbit killed for food.

In Ohlone villages, prayer was an important part of daily life and centered around the Indian's respect for and dependence on nature. Each morning, as the sun rose beyond the hills, the Ohlone went to the doorways of their homes to greet it through prayer. The Indians offered gifts of porridge and seeds to the sun. When the Ohlone smoked tobacco in their pipes, the clouds of smoke were meant as offerings to the sun.

Shamans were the spirtual leaders in Native American communities. Shamans healed the sick and were thought to have the power to control the weather or to cause great harm. Ohlone villagers believed shamans could change themselves into grizzly bears at any time.

Ancestors of the Ohlone had passed down these religious traditions to their children for generations. But the young Ohlone raised at Mission San José learned little about their people's beliefs because the priests forbade the teaching of the old ways.

Neophytes who knew the traditional Ohlone beliefs practiced them in secret. They attended mass and followed the priests' directions only to avoid whippings. Many Indians tried to escape the lifestyle at the missions by running away. Others sought revenge.

Where is discussion of Catholicism?

Runaways and Revolt

Native American groups living east of Mission San José often helped runaway neophytes. Spanish soldiers rode into the Native American villages to find the escapees. Frequently, the soldiers killed or punished Native Americans who were hiding the neophytes. The eastern tribes fought back by taking horses and cattle from the missions and the settlers.

In the fall of 1828, the priests at Mission San José let a neophyte named Estanislao go inland to visit his people. He belonged to the Lacquisamne Yokuts, who lived along the Stanislaus River. Estanislao was a natural commander. At Mission San José, where Estanislao was born and raised, he was given the rank of *alcalde,* or neophyte leader of mission Indians.

During his visit home, Estanislao sent word that he wouldn't be coming back to San José. He had decided to use his leadership skills against the mission.

From his village, Estanislao organized about 500 neophytes from San José and other missions to revolt. Non-mission Native Americans also joined Estanislao.

Father Durán was sure that more neophytes would flee if Estanislao was not brought back to Mission San José. The priest requested more soldiers from the presidio in San Francisco.

A drawing shows Mission San José as it appeared around 1830.

Leatherjacket Soldiers

Some Spanish soldiers in North America were called leatherjackets. These soldiers got the name from their jackets, which were made of seven layers of cowhide or deerskin—leather so thick that arrows couldn't pierce all the way through.

Underneath the jackets, the soldiers' uniforms were cloth, with buckskin coverings for their legs. Bullhide shields protected their left arms from arrows. The soldiers carried short muskets, lances, and broadswords for weapons. Even the horses sported heavy leather covers for their haunches.

In Alta California, most leatherjackets lived at the region's four major presidios, located at San Diego, Monterey, San Francisco, and Santa Barbara. Smaller squads of soldiers were stationed at each of the missions.

The presidios covered about 600 square feet and had 12- to 15-foot-high walls of brick and earth. Each fort contained a chapel, living quarters for the officers, housing for families and soldiers, storehouses, workshops, a well, and a cistern for storing water.

Leatherjackets sometimes carried broadswords, which were large and heavy and had wide blades.

They tracked Estanislao and his followers to Yokuts territory, just east of San Francisco Bay. The troops couldn't drive the Indians from their rocky, heavily wooded shelter. The Native Americans claimed victory after wounding several soldiers and their commander.

During the winter and spring, Estanislao's group fortified its camp. The Indians dug trenches to prevent the soldiers from riding their horses into battle. Estanislao designed a series of stockades (protective fences) and trenches similar to the walls and ditches that protected the presidios. His group took horses, cattle, and supplies from nearby ranches and missions.

Estanislao and his followers believed they could fight off the Spanish soldiers. Because Estanislao had lived at Mission San José, he knew that the soldiers' guns and equipment were old and in need of repair. He also knew that the few hundred

Father Durán called on troops from the presidio at San Francisco to help end Estanislao's Rebellion. Neophytes who revolted were sometimes punished with hard labor at a presidio.

soldiers guarding all the missions and settlers weren't well organized. Because the soldiers often went years without being paid their wages, some of the men were no longer loyal to the government.

In 1829 about 100 troops and neophytes led by a young soldier, Mariano Guadalupe Vallejo, joined forces to overcome Estanislao. The Ohlone in Vallejo's army were traditional enemies of the Yokuts.

When the troops reached Estanislao's stronghold, they set the nearby woods on fire. Cannon balls destroyed two stockades. Exhausted after dodging arrows and battling the heat of the fire, the soldiers retreated. During the night, Estanislao and his followers left. Fighting continued later in different locations. The soldiers killed many Indians, but Estanislao wasn't captured.

After Vallejo's troops had shattered Estanislao's stockades and killed many of his followers, he negotiated an end to the revolt. Estanislao returned to Mission San José, where he was given asylum (protection) by Father Durán. (Traditionally, a Catholic church was considered a sanctuary, or safe place. Soldiers couldn't remove a prisoner from the church without permission from a priest.)

Father Durán wrote to the governor of Alta California asking that Estanislao be forgiven and once again assigned to the mission. The priest argued that, at the mission, Estanislao could be watched. On his own, the Indian leader would be free to provoke more uprisings. The priest hoped that other escaped neophytes would follow Estanislao's example and return to their missions.

No record of the governor's reply has been found, but Estanislao must have received a pardon because he wasn't turned over to the soldiers. Estanislao died years later at Mission San José from smallpox.

Mission San Rafael Arcángel

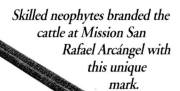

Skilled neophytes branded the cattle at Mission San Rafael Arcángel with this unique mark.

In 1812 Russians established what later became known as Fort Ross, on the coast north of San Francisco Bay. The Russians trapped otters and seals along the Pacific coast for their pelts, which the trappers sold in Europe. They protected their settlement with a large number of cannon.

Fearing that the Russians might try to claim more land, the governor of Alta California wanted a Spanish-speaking settlement located north of San Francisco Bay. He hoped that a settlement might help to prevent the Russians from advancing southward.

Fort Ross was the center of the Russian colony in Alta California. The settlement included ranches, grain fields, and orchards.

Lieutenant Gabriel Moraga, who had explored land north of the bay, suggested a suitable site for a settlement. The spot lay among hills that protected it from Pacific winds. The soil seemed fertile enough to grow fruit, and local grasses could provide pasture for livestock.

The governor suggested that Mission San Francisco de Asís add the land to its holdings and build a hospital on the new grounds. The warmer climate on the north side of the bay would help some of the neophytes. Many of the Native Americans there suffered when the weather turned cold and damp.

Of all the Franciscans in California, Father Luís Gil y Taboada was considered to know the most about medicine. When Father Gil offered to work at the hospital, Father-President Vicente Francisco Sarría agreed to build the structure.

On December 13, 1817, a boatload of soldiers and four

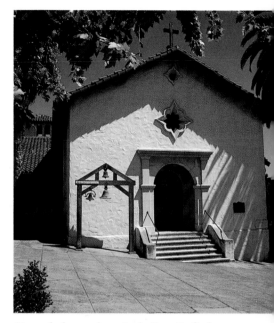

Founded as a hospital, San Rafael Arcángel also had a church.

priests crossed San Francisco Bay. At the site of the new hospital, the missionaries set a cross in place and blessed the land. The following day, the priests baptized 26 Coast Miwok children at the branch mission. The Franciscans named the hospital San Rafael Arcángel, after the angel of good health and healing.

45

Neophytes who had moved from Mission San Francisco de Asís built a church for the branch mission. The plain structure featured bells hanging from a simple redwood frame.

New buildings were added to the church but not in the usual quadrangle shape found at other missions. One building housed the hospital, storehouses, and the priests' quarters. A tule-covered walkway stretched along the outside of the structure.

Native Medicine

The Coast Miwok and the Ohlone had many remedies for pain and illness. They applied jimsonweed, bark, and tobacco to wounds. Shamans crushed plant bulbs to produce a salve for boils and bruises. Healers steeped the bark or leaves of certain plants in hot water, making teas that would relieve cold symptoms, stomach pains, and headaches.

At the missions, some Native Americans used traditional cures. But for the most part, the neophytes were subjected to European medical practices, which at the time were not well developed.

The priests at Mission San Francisco de Asís sent ill neophytes to the hospital at San Rafael. The overall health of the transferred neophytes improved, probably because of the drier climate. In fact, fewer deaths occurred at San Rafael than at any other mission location.

In 1819 Father Gil, sick with heart problems, was sent to another mission to be cared for by Franciscans. Father Juan Amorós came to San Rafael to head the hospital.

Jimsonweed

The Spaniards commonly used a method called "bleeding" to cure a patient. Doctors made a small incision in a patient's vein to take blood. This practice was thought to remove poisons from the body. But often, the technique weakened the ill patient and caused an infection. Many patients suffered even more or died after being bled.

A Deadly Disease

Smallpox, a skin disease, had killed millions of people in Europe, Asia, and Africa before reaching the Indians of California. For centuries, no one knew how to cure the deadly disease. But one thing was for sure—people who survived smallpox never got it again.

Using this information, some people began to take pus from a smallpox blister and place it in a cut made in a healthy person's arm. If all went well, the patient who received the treatment came down with only a mild case of smallpox. If the person was ever exposed to the virus in the future, disease-fighting cells acquired from the treatment would overcome the germs.

Some neophytes at the missions eventually received the treatment. But Native Americans living outside the missions had no resistance to the disease. Traditional methods of healing were useless and sometimes even more harmful. The virus spread quickly and in many cases killed hundreds of Indians in a short period of time.

During mission times, a British scientist developed the first vaccine to fight smallpox. But no treatment was foolproof, and some people who took the vaccine still became ill.

Smallpox victims experienced aches and high fever before getting a rash on their face. The rash, made up of small pimples, eventually spread to other parts of the body. The pus-filled pimples grew larger and formed a scab before falling off. Patients who survived the illness were left with pockmarks.

Father Amorós added to the agricultural worth of San Rafael, which was already valued as a hospital site. He traveled far in search of converts and greatly increased the number of neophytes at San Rafael. Under his supervision, the orchards, vineyards, and fields of the branch mission produced large amounts of fruit and grain.

San Rafael remained part of San Francisco de Asís until 1823. By then, the branch housed about 700 neophytes and was self-sufficient enough to become the twentieth mission.

Mission San Francisco Solano

In 1821 New Spain won its independence from Spain to become the Republic of Mexico. Mexico now ruled over Alta California. The 1822 appointment of a Mexican, Luís Antonio Argüello, as governor of Alta California signaled the end of Spanish influence in the region.

People of different nationalities became a growing part of the population of Alta California. Mexico invited in Mexican soldiers and settlers. Russians still inhabited the north, and people from the United States began to trickle into the territory. By this time, many of the native peoples had died from disease.

In 1823 Father José Altimira, a young priest at Mission San Francisco de Asís, went to Governor Argüello with a plan to close Mission San Francisco de Asís. So many Native Americans near San Francisco had died from disease, the priest argued, that few were left to convert. Altimira proposed that a new Mission San Francisco be built north of San Rafael, where there were more Native Americans to convert to the Catholic faith.

Olives still grow on the grounds of Mission Solano.

The ongoing threat of Russian settlement in the Bay Area worried Governor Argüello and other Mexican officials. Augüello agreed to build the new mission and to close San Francisco de Asís. He also planned to close Mission San Rafael, too. The neophytes at these two missions would move to the new Mission San Francisco.

Father Altimira soon found a promising spot for the new mission in Coast Miwok territory. The site, which was located a few miles northwest of San Pablo Bay, lay near large oak trees and several streams. Elk, antelope, and deer grazed on land suitable for mission cattle. On July 4, 1823, Father Altimira pounded a large cross into the ground at the new location. He returned in August to supervise the building of the mission.

Father-President Sarría, who was ill at the time, grew angry when he learned that Mexican officials had approved the opening of a new mission without bothering to talk to him. Although Alta California now belonged to Mexico, the Franciscans still followed the rules set down long ago by Spain, which had placed the Franciscans in charge of the missions and the neophytes.

Finally, after many letters and conferences, the governor and the new father-president, José Señán, reached an agreement. Missions San Francisco de Asís and San Rafael would stay open.

In addition, to help curb Russian settlement, a twenty-first mission would be added at the northern tip of the California chain, where Father Altimira had placed a cross. Called San Francisco Solano, after a South American missionary, the new Franciscan mission would be the only one built in Alta California after the territory was taken over by Mexico.

Russian Gifts

By 1824 workers had erected a white, wooden church. On April 4, before a crowd of soldiers, workers, and Coast Miwok Indians, Father Altimira dedicated the church.

During the ceremony, 26 Native American children were baptized. By this time, convincing Indians to convert had become easier. Many Indians, robbed of their homelands by ranchos and by missions, had little choice but to seek the shelter of a mission.

The Russians at Fort Ross didn't object to the mission. In fact, they welcomed the new settlement. The Russians were eager

Hides and Tallow

Large herds of cattle grazed the pastures of San Francisco Solano. The meat from the cattle and from wild elk was a major source of food for the people living at the mission.

A section of the mission grounds was set aside for the *matanza,* or slaughter. Workers collected the fat from the slaughtered animals to use for cooking. Some of the hard fat, called tallow, provided the raw material for soap and candles.

Hides from the slaughtered animals were stretched and then staked to the ground to dry. When carefully prepared, hides had many uses. They could be strung across a bed frame to serve as a mattress. Workers shaped the skins into sturdy leather for saddles, shoes, and the seats and backs of chairs. Workers tied beams and rafters to the roofs of buildings with rawhide (hides not softened into leather).

Typical tallow pot

to trade with the missionaries and the Mexicans.

For the dedication, the Russians sent gifts, including altar cloths, religious pictures, vases, bells, candles, and mirrors. Father Altimira brought horses, sheep, cattle, and oxen from Mission San Francisco de Asís.

By the end of 1824, mission buildings at Solano included adobe living quarters for female children, a granary, workshops, a guardhouse, and a barracks. The neophytes planted 160 fruit trees in the church garden. Fences protected trees and corn crops near the church from hungry deer and cattle. The laborers seeded wheat fields and set up a vineyard with 1,000 vines. Livestock roamed grassland within the mission grounds.

Life at the Mission

Father Altimira had a reputation for mistreating the neophytes at San Francisco Solano, personally flogging and imprisoning them. In the fall of 1826, Native Americans who did not belong to the mission attacked it, taking what they could carry and burning some of the buildings. Father Altimira fled and eventually returned to Spain.

Father Buenaventura Fortuni from Mission San José soon arrived at San Francisco Solano.

HE SAID HE DIDN'T KNOW HOW TO CONTROL THEM WITHOUT A WHIP.

He found that most neophytes had abandoned the mission and that only the adobe buildings had survived the fire. With the help of soldiers and a few neophytes, Father Fortuni cleaned up the living quarters and began to rebuild the mission.

Under Father Fortuni's direction, 30 new mission buildings were put up, including an adobe church constructed in 1833. In that year, the aging priest asked to be moved to a mission where he would share the work with another Franciscan.

His replacement, a Mexican named José María Gutiérrez, had difficulty managing the neophytes and often flogged them. Father Gutiérrez claimed that the neophytes no longer attended mass, seldom worked, and often left the mission without permission. He said he didn't know how to control them without a whip.

But by this time, neophytes throughout Alta California had begun to notice many changes taking place at the missions and among Californios. New policies from the government in Mexico had weakened the authority of the Franciscans. In addition, war with the United States was brewing.

PART THREE

Secularization of the Missions

IN THE 1820s AND 1830s, MEXICO FEARED THAT OTHER countries were planning to take over Alta California. In addition to the Russians, traders from Britain, France, and the United States regularly sailed into San Francisco Bay and often visited the missions. Scouting parties from the United States—led by Jedediah Smith and Kit Carson—came overland to Mission San José. John C. Frémont visited Alta California on scientific expeditions. The Mexican government believed that many of these foreigners were spies.

To discourage foreign settlement, Mexican officials tried to increase the number of Mexicans in the region. Convincing Mexicans to move to Alta California, however, was difficult. Along the coast,

Beginning in the early 1800s, foreign ships regularly sailed into San Francisco Bay to trade with the Franciscans, settlers, and Native Americans.

In Ranchero, *a painting by James Walker, the artist shows the strength and pride of the Alta California rancher.*

the Franciscan missions owned the land most suited to farming and ranching.

So the Mexican government began to pass laws to take the large tracts of mission property away from the Franciscans. The land could then be parceled out to Californios, including new Mexican settlers. The policy of having the government take over and redistribute mission property was called secularization.

The government also wanted to release the neophytes from the missions and to give them land, farm tools, and animals. By striving to treat the neophytes fairly, Mexican officials hoped to prevent the Indians from rebelling. Mexico argued that secularization would accomplish what the missionaries had originally intended but had failed to do—to leave the Native Americans in charge of mission property.

Under secularization laws, mission land and buildings were turned over to a civil administrator. The Franciscans could stay at their churches until they were replaced by secular priests— priests who did not perform missionary work. The administrator determined where the Franciscans would live and provided them with food and clothing. The administrators also distributed land, animals, and supplies among the ex-neophytes.

As a new nation, however, Mexico was unstable and tended

to neglect its territories. Mexican soldiers stationed in Alta California, for instance, often went years without pay. The region's governors, civil administrators, and military leaders were sometimes free to interpret secularization laws as they pleased.

A New Life

During secularization, some of the neophytes received supplies, but very few actually got property. Many civil administrators never informed the ex-neophytes of their rights under the laws. Administrators often kept the land for themselves.

Most of the ex-neophytes who did acquire land didn't keep it for long. Californios and other settlers found ways to take it away from the Indians, sometimes by convincing the Indians to sell at very low prices.

The neophytes had faced harsh treatment at the missions, but freedom didn't necessarily make their lives better. Settlers now occupied age-old Ohlone and Coast Miwok homelands. Cattle had overgrazed meadows once visited by deer and other wild animals. The Indians were left with little or no game to

> BETWEEN 1837 AND 1838, ABOUT 65,000 NATIVE AMERICANS DIED FROM A SMALLPOX EPIDEMIC THAT BEGAN NORTH OF SAN FRANCISCO BAY.

hunt. The missions had cut down many of the trees and plowed up the grasslands, destroying plants the Native Americans had used for food and medicine.

Lacking farmland and knowledge of traditional hunting and gathering skills, some of the former neophytes stayed near the missions. This situation forced most ex-neophytes to work on ranchos whose owners often mistreated the Native Americans.

Secularization around the Bay

San Francisco de Asís was among the first missions to be secularized. In 1834 the Franciscans turned the mission over to an administrator. At that time, only about 150 Native Americans still lived there. Most of the neophytes had died from disease or had escaped. In 1838 an outbreak of smallpox killed most of the mission's remaining population.

By the early 1840s, the mission buildings and the presidio in San Francisco were already in poor shape from lack of care. Parts of the mission's quadrangle had been sold or rented to businesses.

I Am Alone

This is a story as told in 1850 by Pedro Alcantara, a Native American at Mission San Francisco de Asís:

"I am very old . . . my people were once around me like the sands of the shore . . . many . . . many. They have all passed away. They have died like the grass . . . they have gone to the mountains. I do not complain, the antelope falls with the arrow. I had a son. I loved him. When the palefaces came he went away. I do not know where he is. I am a Christian Indian, I am all that is left of my people. I am alone."

Father José María Vásquez de Mercado, who was stationed at Santa Clara, occasionally said mass at San Francisco de Asís. In 1846 a secular priest took over its chapel, ending the small role still played by the Franciscans. No record shows that any land or animals were ever given to ex-neophytes.

In 1834 the governor appointed General Mariano Guadalupe Vallejo administrator in charge of Mission San Francisco Solano. Father José Lorenzo Quijas took charge of the old mission church.

Father Quijas traveled between the churches at Missions San Francisco de Asís, San Rafael, and San Francisco Solano. Most of the Spanish missionaries had already died, were ill, or had left. There weren't enough Mexican priests in Alta California to keep all the mission churches open.

During secularization, General Vallejo often found himself in conflict with Father Quijas. They argued over the division of mission property. The governor of Alta California, for example, had granted large tracts of land to Vallejo to repay him for feeding and clothing his troops. As a result, little land was left to be distributed to the Native Americans.

Vallejo did give the ex-neophytes cattle, which non-mission Indians sometimes stole. To stop the raids, Vallejo agreed to manage the livestock at his estate, which was patrolled by soldiers.

Many ex-neophytes found jobs on the ranchos and vineyards of Vallejo's vast estate, which by 1844 had grown to more than 150,000 acres. The livestock-owning Indians received a small share of the profits.

Father Quijas later moved from Solano to San Rafael. Settlers then took Solano's adobe, roof tiles, and wooden beams to use for building their own homes in the nearby town of Sonoma. Without tiles to cover the roof, rain washed away the soft adobe. Everything except the priests' quarters and the adobe chapel was destroyed.

In 1835, when Mission San Rafael was secularized, the administrator in charge gave ex-neophytes some of the mission's horses and sheep and a choice of nearby lands. These Indians decided to settle in Nicasio, a fertile inland valley.

General Vallejo, who was now

A Stranger's House

Father José Quijas had many complaints about the secularization of Mission San Francisco Solano. He was angry about his loss of authority at the mission. In a letter to his superior, Father Quijas wrote:

"It really seems as if I am living in a stranger's house, as everything is closed up and I am forced to have even my little reception room turned into a passageway so that whomever wills may go in and go out . . . . I told [a neophyte] to take out two yoke of oxen; he replied that [he had been given orders] not to obey me anymore in anything I commanded."

in charge of defending northern Alta California, had become a successful and influential leader. As a result, the Mexican government sometimes overlooked the way Vallejo carried out secularization laws.

Under Mexican law, a charge of poor management allowed the government to take land from the Indians. Two years after the Indians moved to Nicasio Valley, Vallejo reclaimed it, reasoning that the Indians had not made good use of the property. General Vallejo said he'd return the land if he ever thought the Indians had learned how to manage it properly.

By 1840 the administrator at San Rafael had given about 190 former neophytes land and livestock. Another 150 Native Americans dwelled nearby. But those who had property found it difficult to keep. Californios and other settlers simply moved onto it.

At Mission Santa Clara, secularization took place in 1836. After the administrator took over, farming and other work practically ceased. Only 300 Native Americans remained at what had once been a well-populated and productive mission. In addition, settlers and Native Americans had stolen most of the mission's sheep and cattle.

Although production at Santa Clara rapidly declined without a large workforce, the mission remained a center of activity. For some years during secularization, the priests at Santa Clara oversaw all the northern mission churches. Mexican soldiers, meanwhile, occupied Santa Clara's buildings.

In 1846 the governor of Alta California, Pío Pico, sold most of the mission's orchards. The priest in charge, Father José Reál, survived by collecting rent from U.S. settlers who wanted to farm plots of the mission's remaining land. The administrator failed to give the ex-neophytes any land.

Pío Pico

General Vallejo's older brother José de Jesus was the administrator of the land and animals at Mission San José, which was secularized in 1836. Soon afterward, government investigators accused José of taking food and clothing from the mission Indians and replaced him with another administrator. José Vallejo denied the charges and claimed that farming flourished under his leadership.

By 1839 the Indian population at San José had dropped by more than 1,300, leaving only about 600 ex-neophytes. Most of the buildings had been robbed of their valuables. In 1846 Governor Pico sold almost all the mission property—except the church and the graveyard—to his brother and to former governor Juan Bautista Alvarado.

The Bear Flag Revolt

In the mid-1830s, border disputes between Mexico and the

John C. Frémont

In this late-nineteenth-century photo, Mariano Guadalupe Vallejo relaxes in front of his home in Sonoma. Even though Vallejo supported a U.S. takeover of Alta California, Bear Flaggers took the retired Mexican general from his home and held him prisoner for several months.

United States caused tension between the two countries. Mexico suspected that the United States was intending to expand its borders all the way to the Pacific Ocean. Some Californios, including General Vallejo, welcomed the idea of being part of a stable nation. Others feared they would lose their land if the United States seized Alta California.

In June 1846, Captain John C. Frémont helped spread rumors that the Mexican army was going to force U.S. settlers to leave Alta California. In protest, more than 30 of these settlers invaded Vallejo's home in the village of Sonoma, near Mission San Francisco Solano.

They told the retired commander that the mission and the pueblo were now part of the Republic of California—a new, independent nation.

They raised a flag in the square near the mission. The flag showed a grizzly bear, drawn with blackberry juice, underlined with a red flannel stripe. A star was placed to the left of the animal on what became known as the Bear Flag. Underneath the picture were the words "Republic of California."

During the revolt, the settlers met with little resistance. The territory lacked a strong military. But the weak Mexican army in Alta California would soon be involved in a more serious struggle.

U.S. Invasion

By the summer of 1846, the United States had declared war on Mexico. The U.S. Navy sailed into California's ports to

The U.S. flag flew over Monterey Bay in 1846 at the start of the Mexican War.

take command of the territory. Commodore John Sloat raised the U.S. flag in Monterey on July 7, 1846.

Few battles of the Mexican War occurred in Alta California. Most of the fighting took place elsewhere in Mexico. In 1848 the United States won the war. Under the Treaty of Guadalupe Hidalgo, Mexico ceded Alta California and other territories

to the United States. In 1850 Alta California, now called simply California, became the thirty-first state.

Meanwhile, Americans had discovered gold in California. Streams of people began arriving from Europe, Asia, South America, and the United States, boosting California's non-native population. The gold seekers boldly started mining land claimed by Native Americans or Californios, and the legal fight for landownership began.

Under Mexican rule, Californios had been granted large tracts of mission property. Because most of the land grants were not well documented, ownership was hard to prove. U.S. settlers simply began ranching and farming on whatever land they wanted.

Under the new state's laws, these people, called squatters, were not required to prove ownership. Many Californios eventually lost their land after expensive court battles. In time, even Californios who succeeded in court gave way to the swelling numbers of squatters.

U.S. ranchers spread into the inland areas, which were still populated with Native Americans. In protest, many Indians stole cattle and horses from the ranchers. Ranchers often killed these Indians, and sometimes their entire villages, in revenge.

In the United States, Indians had few legal rights and could not ask for protection from the ranchers. Indians, in fact, could not even testify in court against white people.

By the late 1800s, the U.S. government had established a number of Indian **reservations** across California. This land, which was set aside as a place for Native Americans to live, was meant to keep Indians and non-Indians apart.

But the quality of reservation land was generally poor for farming or ranching. The Native Americans couldn't make a living off the land and had to rely on the U.S. government for food and other supplies.

In 1849 gold was discovered at Sutter's Mill east of Sacramento, bringing thousands of miners (above) to California. Miwok Indians (top right) harvest wheat for a U.S. farmer in the late 1800s.

61

PART FOUR

The Missions in Modern Times

IN THE 1850s AND 1860s, THE U.S. GOVERNMENT DE-termined that some of the land grants made during secularization were illegal. The government then returned mission buildings and other property to the Roman Catholic Church. But many of the missions had already fallen apart from neglect, and the Church didn't have the funds to repair them.

In the late 1800s, an author named Helen Hunt Jackson published a book called *Ramona*. This fictional story about early California created romantic notions of mission life. Other writings that glorified the era soon followed.

In the late 1800s, artist Edwin Deakin painted San Francisco de Asís and the other 20 missions in a state of decay. His work renewed interest in mission history.

Guadalupe Vallejo, the niece of General Vallejo, grew up on a ranch across the road from Mission San José in the mid-1800s. She wrote the following in a story about her memory of "wash day" and Indian laborers for *Century* magazine in 1890:

"The great piles of soiled linen were fastened on the backs of horses, led by other servants . . . . The girls and women who were to do the washing trooped along by the side of the *carreta* [wooden cart] . . . . A great dark mountain rose behind the hot spring, and . . . columns of white steam rose among the oaks . . . .

"We watched the women unload the linen and carry it to the spring . . . . The women put homemade soap on the clothes, and dipped them in the spring, and rubbed them on the smooth rocks until they were white as snow. Then they were spread out to dry on the tops of the low bushes . . . .

Mexicans in Alta California commonly used the carreta, or wooden cart, to transport people and goods.

" . . . at twilight, the younger children were all asleep in the slow carreta, and the Indians were singing hymns as they drove the linen-laden horses down the dusky ravines."

Stories such as this entertained the public and created an interest in the mission period. Citizens became concerned that the buildings belonging to an important part of California's history had been allowed to decay. People began donating money for mission restoration.

The formation of several private organizations, including the Landmarks Club and the California Historical Landmarks League, led to additional financial assistance. These groups also helped hire laborers to rebuild the crumbling structures.

Mission San Francisco de Asís

After the California gold rush in the mid-1800s, the town of San Francisco grew until it reached Mission San Francisco de Asís. Workers tore down some of the mission buildings, which the church had rented to a tavern and other businesses, to extend Sixteenth Street.

In 1876 workers built a large church next to the mission's original adobe chapel, which had become too small to accommodate the neighborhood's growing population. The mission and its surrounding area became known as the Mission District.

A huge earthquake in 1906 shook the old church bells so hard that they rang. A few tiles fell from the roof, but surprisingly the adobe chapel didn't crumble. Fires raced through the city but were stopped just before reaching San Francisco de Asís. The historic building survived—although the new church was damaged and had to be rebuilt.

The old mission church and a part of the old cemetery are all that remain of the original mission. They sit crowded between

The San Francisco earthquake of 1906 destroyed much of the city, including this area around Market Street. The nearby Mission District, however, was spared much damage.

buildings on Dolores Street. Overshadowed by Mission Dolores Basilica, which was built in 1918 and remodeled in 1926, the old mission chapel is still used for baptisms and other special religious services.

Mission Santa Clara de Asís

In 1851 the Catholic Church turned Mission Santa Clara over to the Jesuit religious order to be

Mission Dolores Basilica (above) towers over the neighboring adobe chapel, which was built in 1791. The cemetery at San Francisco de Asís (right) includes the graves of Franciscans and neophytes. A statue of Father Junípero Serra sits in the middle.

The remains of a wall (above) built by the neophytes at Santa Clara partially line the quadrangle. The bell tower (above right) in the chapel at the University of Santa Clara contains an original mission bell dated from 1793.

used as a private college. Teachers held classes in the remains of the mission buildings. In 1912 the institution became the University of Santa Clara.

Architects designed the campus around the mission buildings. Many of the old structures were changed for practical reasons. The roof of the church, for example, was widened to help protect the decaying adobe walls from heavy rains. Eventually, wood replaced the adobe.

In 1926 a sudden fire destroyed the old mission church. Students, priests, and firefighters rescued a few of the items in the structure, including several statues. A bell that had been a gift from King Carlos IV of Spain in 1798 was spared and hangs in the latest chapel, which was built in 1929.

The campus of the University of Santa Clara is open to students and visitors. The chapel still holds regular services.

Mission San José de Guadalupe

In 1858 the U.S. govenment returned the crumbling adobe structures of Mission San José to the Catholic Church. On October 21, 1868, a strong tremor shifted and collapsed the buildings. Only a small section of the quadrangle was left standing.

In 1869 the priest at San José built a new church from redwood over the old mission floor. In 1982 volunteers raised money to rebuild the mission church as it had originally looked. Workers moved the wooden church, and archaeologists searched the site for information about the old mission chapel.

The archeologists found thousands of artifacts, including bits of glass, scraps of lumber, and

The interior of the church at Mission San José has been rebuilt to look as it did in the early 1800s.

pieces of the chandeliers. These items helped the team of workers reconstruct the mission.

After architects finished the plans, builders poured cement on top of the rock foundation that the neophytes had laid. Steel-reinforced walls lined the new building to help support it during earthquakes. All modern

A metal baptismal font, or bowl, buried under the ruins of Mission San José was uncovered and placed in the reconstructed church. During mission times, Franciscans filled the font with holy water to baptize the Indians.

As in mission times, rawhide secures the mission bells at San José.

necessities, such as the public address system, were hidden from view.

Eighteenth-century window glass was found in junkyards and cut to size. Uneven and bubbled, the glass resembled the windows in the original church. Artisans hand made hinges, doors, and other building materials to match the originals.

Artists Huu Van Nguyen and Richard Menn carefully painted the walls of the new mission church with the same images believed to have once covered the old church. Menn, who designed the altars, spent four years finding the right materials.

He gathered decorations from old missions in Europe and Mexico. Some pieces were discovered locally. In a gift shop in

Not far from Mission San José is an Ohlone cemetery, the resting place of the neophytes who built and worked at the mission. The Galvan family, descendents of neophytes who lived at Mission San José, care for the graves.

Carmel, California, for example, Menn found a Spanish statue of Saint Joseph made in 1600.

A priest dedicated the new mission church on June 11, 1985. This day marked the 188th anniversary of the planting of the cross at Mission San José by Father Fermín de Lasuén.

Mission San Rafael Arcángel

Soon after secularization, the buildings of Mission San Rafael Arcángel began to fall apart. The church was abandoned in 1842. Four years later, the Mexican government granted the mission to settlers. In 1855 the U.S. government returned San Rafael to the Catholic Church.

Settlers had carted off the usable parts of the buildings—adobe bricks, roof tiles, and beams—to be used for other structures. In 1870 the priests had the crumbling church taken down. San Rafael became the only mission to have been completely destroyed over time. In the late 1800s, no part of the original structure remained at the site.

Workers built a new mission chapel in 1949 on the mission grounds. It faces the hills, whereas the original mission church looked out toward the bay.

Mission San Francisco Solano

By the 1880s, Mission San Francisco Solano was in ruins. The Catholic Church had sold the property to a private individual and had used the money to build a new church for the nearby town of Sonoma. The owner stored hay and wine in the old buildings until the California Historical Landmarks League bought the mission in 1903. The organization then began to reconstruct the mission buildings.

The San Francisco earthquake of 1906 damaged some of the mission. Repairs were made in 1911 and again in the 1940s. Some original items, such as the

Old church items, including a picture of San Rafael Arcángel, are on display at the mission.

church bells, were found and placed in the new church. Chandeliers made to look like those from the mission period, an oil painting of San Francisco Solano, and paintings similar to those made by the neophytes were added during restoration.

The mission buildings are now part of the Sonoma Mission State Historic Park and are open to tourists. The inside of the church is not an exact copy of the original mission chapel but looks like many of the mission churches planned by the Franciscans. The only original building left from the old mission quadrangle is a section of the priests' quarters.

Bay Area Native Americans Today

Native peoples in the Bay Area also experienced many changes. By the mid-1800s, several Indian groups, including the Ohlone, were thought to have died out.

The chapel at San Francisco Solano (below) is plainer than those built during the height of the mission period. A table and bed (right) used by the Franciscans sit in a room of the priests' quarters.

Protest on Alcatraz

In 1969 Native Americans in the Mission District of San Francisco were planning a major protest. In that year—not far from the old Spanish missions—300 people from around the nation seized an abandoned prison on the rocky island of Alcatraz in San Francisco Bay.

Alcatraz, known as Diamond Island by the Ohlone, had once been part of Ohlone territory. According to Ohlone legend, only animals—not humans—were meant to occupy Alcatraz. For this reason, the Ohlone and the Coast Miwok refused to participate in the event.

Most of the activists, who called themselves the Indians of All Tribes, were not natives of California and were probably unaware of the legend. They set up a fictional reservation for white people, pledging to teach them Native American religion and lifeways.

The takeover of Alcatraz illustrated to many non-Indians how government policies—whether Spanish, Mexican, or American—must have affected the Indians. Some activists stayed on the island until 1971, when U.S. government agents peaceably removed the protestors.

As part of the protest on Alcatraz Island, a Native American painted the words "Indian American Land" on the wall of a former prison building.

Descendants of the Ohlone, however, still live near San Francisco Bay. Nearly 150 years after California became a state, Ohlone groups are still seeking recognition from the U.S. government. Ohlone people want at least to be paid for the lands that were taken from their ancestors.

Likewise, few Coast Miwok survive, and their language is no longer in use. Many of the people who claim to be at least part Coast Miwok belong to other tribes or have married non-natives. Nevertheless, the group hopes to revive its culture and to prove its existence to the U.S. government.

Both the Coast Miwok and the Ohlone, along with other California Indians, are working to have memorials put up at every mission site. The memorials would list the names of the thousands of Indians now buried in unmarked mass graves that surround the missions. This effort to honor the neophytes would also serve to remind visitors that Native Americans were the builders of the Spanish missions of California.

Herds of elk no longer graze on mission grounds. Towering grizzlies cannot be found feasting on the berries and acorns that once grew in abundance around the great bay. The Ohlone and the Coast Miwok don't fill the mission churches to repeat their prayers in Latin.

Most of the mission fields and grazing lands have been covered with cement, roads, and houses. But smoke still rises from homes on a cold day, just as it did from Ohlone and Coast Miwok villages. The smoke drifts upward to the sun, which still marks the time of day and the seasons.

A tribal elder of the Muwekma Ohlone sits with two of her great-grandchildren.

73

slanted

AFTERWORD

Each year thousands of tourists and students visit the California missions. Many of these visitors look around and conclude that the missions are the same today as they were long ago. But, over time, the missions have gone through many changes. The earliest structures were replaced by sturdier buildings with tall towers and long arcades. But even these solid buildings eventually fell into ruin and later were reconstructed.

Our understanding of the missions also has changed through the years. Missionaries, visitors, novelists, and scholars have expressed different opinions about the California missions. These observers often have disagreed about the impact of the missions on the Indians in California. And the voices of Native Americans—from the past *and* the present—have continued to shed light on the mission experience.

The early Franciscan missionaries believed that they were improving the local Indians by introducing them to mission life. But visitors from Europe and the United States frequently described the Spanish missions as cruel places. A French explorer in 1786, for example, reported that the priests treated the neophytes like slaves. He was horrified that Spanish soldiers tracked down runaway Indians and whipped them for trying to return to their old way of life.

Many early visitors were truly concerned about the mistreatment of Native Americans. But the foreign travelers, jealous of Spain's hold on Alta California, also criticized the missions as a way to prove that Spain wasn't worthy to possess the region. Similarly, a young man from the eastern United States, visiting Alta California in the 1830s, was saddened to see so much sickness and death at the missions. He advised his fellow Americans that the region would fare much better as a part of the United States.

The missions were all but forgotten during the 25 years following the U.S. takeover of California. The once solid structures decayed into piles of rotting adobe. One U.S. visitor wrote that she doubted if any structure on earth was "colder, barer, uglier, [or] dirtier" than a California mission.

Just when the missions had disappeared almost completely, they came roaring back to public attention. Beginning in the 1880s, dozens of novels and plays about early California described the Franciscan priests as kind-hearted souls who treated neophytes with gentleness and care. This favorable image of the missions became popular because it gave many Californians a positive sense of their own history and identity. The writings also attracted droves of tourists to California. Merchants and business leaders in the state supported the rebuilding of the crumbling missions because it made good business sense.

The missions today are still the subject of a lively debate. Some people continue to believe that the missions brought many benefits to the Indians by "uplifting" them to European ways. But many others, including some descendants of the neophytes, say that the missions destroyed Native American lifeways and killed thousands of Indians. For all of us, the missions continue to stand as reminders of a difficult and painful time in California history.

Dr. James J. Rawls
Diablo Valley College

CHRONOLOGY

Important Dates in the History of the Missions of the San Francisco Bay Area

1500s	Spanish and English explorers land in what is now California
1769	San Diego de Alcalá, the first Franciscan mission in Alta California, is established; Gaspar de Portolá finds San Francisco Bay
1776	Anza expedition reaches San Francisco Bay and settlers begin building Yerba Buena; San Francisco de Asís is dedicated; San Francisco Presidio is founded
1777	Mission Santa Clara and Pueblo San José de Guadalupe are founded
1784	Father Junípero Serra dies; Fermín Francisco de Lasuén becomes the new father-president
1797	Mission San José de Guadalupe is established
1810	Revolution begins in New Spain
1812	Russians build Fort Ross
1817	San Rafael Arcángel opens hospital
1821	New Spain gains independence from Spain
1823	San Francisco Solano, the twenty-first and last Franciscan mission in Alta California, is founded
1828-29	Estanislao's Rebellion
1830s	Missions are secularized
1846	Bear Flag Revolt; Mexican War begins; U.S. Navy occupies Alta California
1848	Mexican War ends; Mexico cedes Alta California to the United States
1850	California becomes the thirty-first state
1850s	U.S. government begins to return the California missions to the Catholic Church; mission buildings are falling apart
1890s- present	Missions are restored

ACKNOWLEDGMENTS

Photos, maps, and artworks are used courtesy of: Laura Westlund, pp. 1, 13, 19, 30, 34, 37, 38, 44, 48; © Lynda Richards pp. 2–3, 66 (right), 67 (right); Southwest Museum, Los Angeles, CA, pp. 8–9 (photo by Don Meyer, CT.374–646.G136); North Wind Picture Archives, pp. 10–11, 12, 64; © Jo-Ann Ordano, pp. 15, 22; © Carol Stiver, pp. 16–17, 45 (right); Bancroft Library, pp. 18 (left), 21, 24, 27, 31, 43, 54, 59 (left and right); © Frank S. Balthis, pp. 18 (right), 20, 69 (right); California Historical Society, Title Insurance and Trust Photo Collection, Dept. of Special Collections, Univ. of Southern California Library, p. 23; IPS, pp. 25 (left and right), 32, 33, 60; © Ron Bohr, pp. 28–29, 66 (left), 71 (bottom); © Diana Petersen, pp. 30, 35, 67 (left), 68, 69 (left), 71 (top); U.S. Dept. of Agriculture, p. 36; Collection of the Oakland Museum of California, Museum of Donors' Acquisition Fund, p. 40; The Bettmann Archive, p. 41; Museum of New Mexico (neg. #147832), p. 42; © Chuck Place, pp. 45 (left), 49, 70; © Eda Rogers / Sea Images, p. 46; Department of Library Services, American Museum of Natural History (neg. #4051), p. 47; © Diane C. Lyell, p. 50; Historic Urban Plans, pp. 52–53; Huntington Library, p. 58; National Cowboy Hall of Fame and Western Heritage Center, Oklahoma City, p. 61 (left); California State Library, p. 61 (right); Seaver Center for Western History Research, Natural History Museum of Los Angeles, pp. 62–63; Library of Congress, p. 65; UPI / Bettmann, p. 72; Muwekma Ohlone Tribe of the San Francisco Bay Area, p. 73; IPS / Nancy Smedstad, pp. 74–75; Tekla N. White, p. 78 (top); Dr. James J. Rawls, p. 78 (middle); Professor Edward D. Castillo, p. 78 (bottom); Cover: (Front) © Diana Petersen; (Back) Laura Westlund.

Quotations are from the original translated writings or statements of Father José Bernardo Sánchez, p. 37; Pedro Alcantara (as recorded by Adam Johnson), p. 56; and Father José Quijas, p. 57. The quotation on p. 64 is reprinted by permission of Roy E. Kern.

METRIC CONVERSION CHART

WHEN YOU KNOW	MULTIPLY BY	TO FIND
inches	2.54	centimeters
feet	0.3048	meters
miles	1.609	kilometers
square feet	0.0929	square meters
acres	0.4047	hectares
ounces	28.3495	grams
pounds	0.454	kilograms
gallons	3.7854	liters

ABOUT THE AUTHOR

Tekla N. White, a freelance writer, taught elementary school for 28 years before retiring in 1994. She has written social science materials for teachers and students. Her newspaper and magazine articles have covered a variety of subjects, including fleas, apples, and braces. Her interest in Hispanic and Native American cultures began at the University of Washington. Ms. White, who has earned degrees in English writing and Spanish literature, has also studied archaeology and anthropology and is fluent in Spanish. Born in Portland, Oregon, Ms. White currently lives in Fremont, California, near Mission San José. She is a member of the Society of Children's Book Writers and Illustrators.

ABOUT THE CONSULTANTS

James J. Rawls is one of the most widely published and respected historians in the field of California history. Since 1975 he has been teaching California history at Diablo Valley College. Among his publications are *Indians of California: the Changing Image, New Directions in California History,* and, with Walton Bean, *California: An Interpretive History.* Dr. Rawls is also the author of several works for young readers, including *Never Turn Back: Father Serra's Mission* and *California Dreaming.* Dr. Rawls frequently serves as a consultant for books, for television and radio programs, and for film documentaries on subjects dealing with California's history.

Edward D. Castillo is a direct descendant of Cahuilla-Luiseño Indians who lived at Missions San Gabriel and San Luis Rey. A professor of California Indian ethnohistory for more than 20 years, Castillo offers Native perspectives of mission life to students of California history. His first book is entitled *Native American Perspectives on the Hispanic Colonization of Alta California.* He recently cowrote, with historian Robert Jackson, *Indians, Franciscans and Spanish Colonization: The Impact of the Mission System on California Indians.* Professor Castillo is a founding member of the Native American Studies Departments at the Los Angeles and Berkeley campuses of the University of California. At Sonoma State University, he serves as an associate professor and chairs its Native American Studies Department.

INDEX